KARATE POWER!

LEARNING THE ART OF THE EMPTY HAND

George R. Parulski, Jr. with

Frankie "Dr. Speed" Mitchell and the East Coast Demo Team

Foreword by Fumio Demura, Technical Advisor, THE KARATE KID
Introduction by Dan Ivan, Technical Assistant, THE KARATE KID

CONTEMPORARY
BOOKS, INC.
CHICAGO

Library of Congress Cataloging in Publication Data

Parulski, George R.
  Karate power! learning the art of the open hand.

  Includes index.
  1. Karate.   I. Mitchell, Frankie.   II. Title.
GV1114.3.P37   1985   796.8'153   85-5946
ISBN 0-8092-5295-3

Cover and interior photography by George R. Parulski, Jr.

Published by Contemporary Books, Inc.
180 North Michigan Avenue, Chicago, Illinois 60601
Manufactured in the United States of America
Library of Congress Catalog Card Number: 85-5946
International Standard Book Number: 0-8092-5295-3

Published simultaneously in Canada by Beaverbooks, Ltd.
195 Allstate Parkway, Valleywood Business Park
Markham, Ontario L3R 4T8 Canada

This book is humbly dedicated to the following people:

Bill "Rocket Man" Rourke
Rob "The Gentleman" Horowitz
Kurt "Killer" Carlson
Peter "The Rock" Manfredi
Chris "Chop Suey" Parker

True followers, walking the path of *budo*!

and

To Mom,
Thank You for Everything!

CONTENTS

FOREWORD BY FUMIO DEMURA

Dear George R. Parulski, Jr.:

Congratulations again on another martial arts book that should indeed be a winner. I am especially pleased with the positive influence this book on karate should have on our young people. After reviewing the material, I find it presented in an excellent way. The writing is crisp and the photos clear and precise.

Young people represent the future of karate, as well as our society. It is important to instill the discipline of karate at a young age in order to help one grow to full maturity as both an adult and a karateka. Your excellent text should become the "Bible of Karate" for the young adult.

Sincerely yours,

Fumio Demura
Chief Director
Japan Karate Federation of America
Headquarters: Santa Ana, California

Technical Advisor
The Karate Kid movie

PREFACE BY DOUG IVAN

Karate Power, Learning the Art of the Open Hand, is a clear, concise summary of the basic to intermediate techniques in the art of karate. George R. Parulski, Jr., continues the long tradition of elaborating on and clarifying the teachings of this ancient martial way. Unlike other texts that have been written in the past on karate aimed at the young adult, Parulski has left no stone unturned. He presents in one easy-to-read volume all the important basic techniques in Japanese karate. He does this with chapters on hand techniques, kicking methods, kata practice, and even signs-of-the-times techniques such as creative sparring techniques (presented by the East Coast Demo Team).

To the beginner, this book will be a guide on the path to true karate fulfillment. For the specialist, this book makes available such a wide range of interest that there is something in it for everyone. The traditionalist will enjoy the attention to detail as well as the presentation of the classical shotokan *gankaku* kata. For the eclectic practitioner, the mixing of break dancing with karate techniques should prove interesting. For the philosopher, it provides insights into history, theory, and techniques written in language our young people can understand and appreciate.

It is perhaps the most readable book I have found on karate for its age audience. It includes what is important and presents it so the reader can understand it. It is certainly far and away the best book available on karate for the young adult today.

Doug Ivan
Chief of Operations
United States Branch
International Martial Arts Federation
(Kokusai Budo Renmei)

Fight Scenes Coordinator
The Karate Kid movie

INTRODUCTION BY DAN IVAN

When walking the path of karate, one soon learns that it is a very difficult and frustrating experience: to learn and to continue to practice it! However, in the same light, karate training can be the most important thing you will ever do in your life. Karate trains your body to perfection and develops a sound mental character as well. The by-products of karate training are many, but perhaps two of the most important are self-discipline and self-defense. After almost four decades of integration into our society—including its acceptance into most of the major universities and colleges in our country—karate has indeed arrived! Thousands upon thousands of karate enthusiasts, students, disciples, and black belt graduates attest to karate's positive impact on their lives. For everyone from very young preschoolers to older family men, karate helps them overcome the daily problems that we all face. Your age, your sex, even your physical condition does not really matter in karate. There is room for everyone!

There are techniques and things to learn that even those who are physically impaired can master. The by-products of true *karate-do* ("the way of karate") are speed, agility, improved coordina-tion, and, *most important,* a sound mind and character. Remember, in karate, your biggest opponent is yourself. It is constant training to achieve higher levels of skill that helps you develop into the person you want to be. Your training partners are there to help contribute to your development: they help you help yourself. These are lessons that can be related directly to all walks of life: home, school, and play!

Karate is a word that translates from the Japanese to mean "the empty hand." This implies that you face the world weaponless yet fearless. Karate had its origins in China and India and then spread to the tiny island of Okinawa; from there it reached its state of perfection in Japan. Thus, although each country has a slightly different version of karate (and they call it by different names, such as *taekwon-do, kung-fu, kenpo,* etc.), the end result is the same. It is like taking many different paths up the mountainside. Each path is different, yet each one reaches the top.

American servicemen, stationed in the Far East after World War II, were among the first to be exposed to karate. The greatest exposure was in Japan, where slowly the secrets of these ancient arts were unveiled to the foreigners. Americans and those of other nationalities began to have a new respect for their former enemies, the Japanese. Through karate and other martial arts training, many barriers between the Japanese and Americans were broken: the hostilities and suffering of the past war were diminished. Karate and judo were the most popular of the martial arts for Americans, followed then by aikido, jujutsu, kendo, and other lesser-known arts.

Returning Americans established martial arts schools of their own in the United States, and by the '60s and '70s the art of karate had spread to every state in the union.

Karate is a part of the samurai *bushido*, a fighting code of the Japanese warrior that stressed respect and loyalty for authority. The Japanese word *budo* means "fight ways." Karate is budo, but the concept goes far deeper than the learning of fighting ways. It means learning the skills of fighting so that you will never have to resort to fighting. With karate or budo training, you become strong enough *not* to fight.

The sport of karate is also becoming very popular in our modern times, although the ancient masters did not intend it to be a sport. In sport karate you apply your techniques against an opponent with controlled movements. A referee or judge awards you points to decide on the winner; but above all, in sport, *contact* with or injury to your opponent is not allowed. It must be remembered that the basis of karate is always self-defense, and its sometimes intricate movements were conceived by the masters for only that purpose. Respect, courtesy, and honor are absolutely necessary to learning karate. Without them, you can never achieve the highest state of mind that truly transforms a person into one with the enlightened goals of budo.

This book, by Sensei George Parulski, Jr., is one of the best ever directed to our young people. In fact, anyone, irrespective of age or sex, will find it totally informative and fascinating.

Dan Ivan
U.S. Representative
Japan Karate Federation
Black Belt: Karate, Judo, Aikido

ACKNOWLEDGMENTS

The author wishes to express his sincere thanks to the following people and organizations: To Jody Rein, my editor at Contemporary Books, Inc., who came up with the idea of doing a karate book for young people. To Frankie "Dr. Speed" Mitchell and his East Coast Demo Team, for appearing in the majority of the photos in this book. To Debbie Mazzochetti and her school, Mazzochetti Karate, Ltd., for appearing in a good portion of the photos. To Randy Pumputis of the Pumputis Karate Academy, whose students appear on the cover of this book. To Dan Ivan of the Japan Karate Federation, for his informative foreword and his kind words and suggestions. And to Rich Russell of Russell Photography, who did all black-and-white processing of the photos in this book. Thank you, one and all.

PART I
GETTING STARTED

1

THE HISTORY OF KARATE

Many years ago, in China, a small old man with a long white beard was walking through the woods, leaning on a gnarled walking stick. At a turn in the path he was confronted by three bandits. They had already attacked one man—he was lying on the ground—and now their attention was turned to him.

"Go away, old man. Mind your own business. This matter does not concern you!" commanded the leader of the bandits.

Calmly the old man replied, "Don't you know that the affairs of one man are the concern of all men? What you do to him affects me."

"Stop preaching, old man, or I'll smash you like this," said the huge bandit leader as he kicked over a small tree.

The old man smiled faintly. "I do not fear you. Nor do I fear what you think you can do to me. Again I say, leave the man alone!"

With that, the headstrong leader lost his temper and kicked at the head of the old man. Without effort, the old man sidestepped the kick and swept the bandit's support leg out from under him. The huge leader fell to the ground.

The second bandit—a tall, wiry woman with piercing eyes—drew her sword and rushed toward the old man. She slashed at his head, but before the blade found its mark the old man had stepped out of the way. The woman turned around to see the third bandit, who was trying to wrestle with the old man, go flying through the air and land in a big puddle of mud.

The three bandits, now outraged at their humiliation, growled, cursed, and attacked the old man all at once. But the little man could not be touched. The three bandits were tossed about like paper dolls until eventually all three landed in a heap, one on top of the other.

Realizing they were in the presence of a master, the three dropped to their knees and begged the old man to forgive them. "Make us your students, please. Teach us to fight!"

"I cannot teach you any fighting art," said the old man. "My art is not a way of fighting. It is for the good of the character and the body. What I can teach you is a way of peace. If you are interested in this, come with me."

The story goes that the three bandits followed our hero into the forest. Although history does not account for the lives of the three bandits, we do know that the master was a kung-fu master of the Shaolin monastery. Around the year A.D. 520, he and other monks and nuns of that order—some of the greatest fighters of their time—developed the fighting arts in ways never attempted before and in a manner that strongly influenced the martial arts as we know them today.

According to legend, about 1,500 years ago, an Indian monk by the name of Bodhidharma traveled from India to China, walking alone across the dangerous Himalayan mountains, through forests filled with wild animals, through swamps, and even over unbridged rivers. His quest: to bring to China the teaching of a new religion called Zen Buddhism.

Bodhidharma eventually arrived at the Shaolin monastery in the Honan province. This monastery was called *shaolin* ("young forest") because the monastery was hidden way in the middle of a huge pine forest. Here Bodhidharma began to teach the young monks his new way of Buddhism. However, he found that the monks were so weak from their inactive life in the monastery that they would fall asleep during the meditations he was trying to teach them. So Bodhidharma taught them a series of special exercises to make them healthy and strong, reminding them that they could never be spiritually strong if they were physically weak.

This philosophy, as well as these special exercises, laid down the foundations of a method of fighting that came to be called *kung-fu*.

Through this training the monks developed good balance and very strong legs. They discovered that they were no longer helpless when they were attacked by bandits who traveled the countryside. Their balance was so good and their legs so rooted to the ground that the bandits could not easily push them around. That is why the old monk in our story could not be pushed down.

With this disciplined training the monks developed such good concentration and such keen awareness of their surroundings that sometimes they had a sixth sense about things. If they were attacked by bandits, for example, they could almost see what the bandits were going to do before they moved. And the months of pain and struggle with Bodhidharma's exercises had made them tough enough to hold up under the pressure of actual fighting situations. It was this training, coupled with the meditation of Zen Buddhism, that gave the old man in our story such sharp awareness of his enemies' movements and made him so calm in the face of danger.

As the years passed the monks devised new and better ways of fighting. They refined the ancient hand-to-hand fighting methods that often used to require brute strength. The new approaches, developed mostly by trial and error, used faster, more effective movements aimed at getting the best results with the smallest amount of effort. These new methods were applied against vital points ("pressure points") on the body, making it possible for the very small to defeat the very big.

Fortunately for us, these new concepts did not remain hidden in the green forests of Honan province. The training methods spread to other Shaolin orders (in the Fukien, Wu Tang, Omei, Kwang-tung provinces). Their fame spread, and people from all over China hoped to get accepted into a Shaolin order. Monks and nuns traveled throughout their country, which was in the middle of a civil war and filled with bandits. They taught the people Shaolin fighting styles so they could defend themselves, and they spread Zen Buddhist teachings to bring peace to China. In this way, Shaolin fighting spread across China, where it was refined and expanded by other masters over the years.

In time, people trained in fighting ways traveled to Korea, Japan, and Okinawa, spreading their philosophy and martial arts knowledge. It is in this way that fighting arts entered the tiny island of Okinawa, where karate was born.

KARATE IS BORN

Karate came to Okinawa around A.D. 1379, when the Chinese, trained in kung-fu, began exchange programs so the two countries could learn about each other's culture. However, the art never really caught on until the powerful Satsuma clan from Japan banned weapons in 1609. Soldiers were sent out to collect knives, spears, and even rusty swords from the people of the small island.

The proud Okinawans, who wanted to get rid of the Satsumas and needed protection from outlaws and bandits, began to develop secret ways of fighting. Lacking swords and spears, the Okinawans began to develop methods using their hands and feet.

The Okinawans searched into their own past for native fighting arts and at the same time began to take more seriously the Chinese kung-fu that had come to the island hundreds of years before. They mixed their native fighting art, called *tode*, with Chinese kung-fu and developed an art called *Okinawa-te*. *Te* meant "hand," and *Okinawa-te* meant "Okinawan hand."

Sometimes the Okinawans also called their combat methods *kara-te*. *Kara* was the word referring to the T'ang dynasty of China, and *kara-te* essentially meant "Chinese hand," which shows how important the role China played in Okinawa's martial arts culture was.

Over the years, three major schools of karate, centered in three different Okinawan cities, developed: *shuri-te*, from the city of Shuri; *naha-te*, from the city of Naha; and *tomari-te*, from the city of Tomari. The Shuri style supposedly was related directly to the Shaolin temple in China. The Naha system seems to have developed from the Wutang school in China, named after the Chinese mountain where it was practiced. The Tomari school was a combination of both Shuri and Naha.

The father of modern karate is Gichin Funakoshi. Funakoshi was born in Shuri in 1868 and was a very small, sick child. So Funakoshi's father started teaching him the *shuri-te* style at the age of 13.

After studying karate for some time, Funakoshi got stronger, tougher, and healthier. This made him take his training more seriously. Because he was truly interested and stuck to it,

Funakoshi became a highly skilled *karateka* (karate practitioner) and eventually began to teach karate in the Okinawan school system.

In 1923, Funakoshi went to Japan to demonstrate karate for judo and ju-jutsu people. The Japanese were so impressed by his skill that he was invited to stay in Japan and teach his art. Karate became a standard part of Japanese life. So much so that, in 1930, Funakoshi made a change in the word *kara-te* to reflect this growing "Japanization." He altered the Chinese writing of *kara* (Which meant "T'ang") to mean "empty." So karate became the "way of the empty hand."

Karate has spread to all parts of the world, including the United States. In our country alone, there are about four million practitioners of karate, the largest group being young people.

CODE OF CONDUCT FOR YOUNG KARATE STUDENTS

1. I promise I will always conduct myself in a dignified manner, remembering the ideals of humility, truth, and honor.

2. I will always strive for the highest standards of cleanliness, and I will make sure that my friends and family do the same.

3. I will always be ethical and honest in my educational as well as my business practices so I never mar the image of a martial artist.

4. I promise always to respect others and to strive for my greatest potential as a human being.

2

THE WORLD OF KARATE:
GETTING TO KNOW THE INS AND OUTS

Like any specialized field, karate has its own set of terms, customs, and special techniques that make it stand on its own, separate from, yet a part of, American life.

The moment you enter the *dojo*, or training hall, you'll see that karate is a world of its own. Shoes are taken off and never worn in the workout area. The insides of most karate schools are the same, usually very simple, with a bare or carpeted floor. When students enter, they change into their karate uniforms, called *gi*—pajamalike tops and loose pants tied with drawstrings. These uniforms make everyone in the class look similar and are loose enough so that students can move freely. From this moment on, students enter the world of karate.

So that you can learn more about the art, the following pages answer common questions about the myths, lore, and customs of karate.

Q. *I've seen people break boards and bricks with their bare hands. Is this stuff real?*

A. While it is true that breaking objects—called *tameshiwara*—is an important part of some styles of karate, it is not something you are likely to learn in training because boards and bricks don't strike back. Why, then, would people break them? They do so primarily for demonstration purposes—to show the true power of karate. In this sense, the feats of breaking you see are *very real*!

In order to break an object successfully, you must condition your hands through training called *makiwara*. This method of conditioning strengthens the knuckles and palm edge of the hand, getting it used to the impact it receives during a breaking demo. Since this is a very specialized part of karate, very few people follow it today.

Q. *Are boys better at karate than girls?*

A. Karate is designed so that anyone, of any size, shape, age, or sex, can practice the art successfully. Power does not depend on body structure; it comes from using correct karate principles. In the past, the activity certainly was dominated by men, but recently—during the 1970s and 1980s—more and more women have been achieving status in the art. So much so that many women are considered superior to men in karate. When you read the word *karateka*, you should picture both men and women, as well as girls and boys.

Q. *If karate power does not depend on size, shape, or sex, what is the secret to developing karate power?*

A. The secret of karate power lies in following certain principles of proper technique—using one's mind, spirit, and body in just the right way.

One of the most important principles is called *focusing*, or *kime* in Japanese. This principle is used in all karate punching, striking, blocking, and kicking. If there is one secret to karate, it is this force of relaxing and tensing. It is this special coordination of mind and body that makes karate different from street fighting.

Example: When throwing a karate punch (see Chapter 4), you put your whole body behind it. As your hand is extended in the punching motion, your arm is kept soft and relaxed. At the moment of impact, the arm tenses, giving the punch a whipping action. This whiplike power is *kime*.

Q. *Why do people shout in karate practice?*

A. This shouting is called *kiai*. A *kiai* usually is done simultaneously with the actions of focusing (*kime*). The yelling helps the karateka (karate practitioner) focus his energy. More than this, the yell itself can have a powerful effect against opponents. It is said that some masters could actually leave opponents dead in their tracks with their *kiai*.

Kiai means more than yelling. In essence, it brings forth the body's energy (called *ki*). To *kiai* is to focus your *ki* in a technique, giving it all you've got.

Q. *Why are there different-colored belts in karate?*

A. Many different martial arts systems—judo, taekwon-do, ju-jutsu, etc.—make use of the belt system, with the highest rank usually being the black belt. Where did the idea of the black belt come from?

According to one story, the idea came from China. When the Chinese people first began studying various fighting arts, they trained in grassy fields near their homes. Students sometimes wore white outfits tied with white sashes or belts. From the many falls and rolls they took on the ground their uniforms became green with grass stains. People washed the uniforms often, but not the belts. Soon, belts became greener and greener.

When the grass wore out under the constant training, the uniforms began to get soiled in dirt and the belts just kept getting darker. When the student had trained a long time, his belt became black with wear.

Over the years, the black belt has become the symbol for an advanced beginner—not an *expert*, as some might think. There are various levels of black belt. The lowest is 1st degree (called *shodan*), and the highest is usually 10th degree (*judan*). The black belts make up a series of degrees called *dan* ranks. Before you can achieve a *dan* rank, you must pass through the colored belts called *kyu*. In some ways, the *kyu* ranks are like elementary school, 1st-degree black belt is like high school, and the higher *dans* are like college.

Q. *What is a karate class like?*

A. While the actions of the students, the design of the *dojo* (gym), and the exact class content may differ from school to school, the average karate class would go something like this:

Before they step into the *dojo* itself, students bow as a sign of respect for the area. At the start of class, students line up according to rank. Then, on the command of the *sensei* (teacher), all students kneel in order of their rank—the higher belts first and the lower belts last. At this point the teacher will shout, "Zazen." This is a command to kneel and meditate. During meditation, the students try to empty their minds. This means to forget everything except karate practice, which allows students to concentrate better.

The instructor and students bow to each other with a *zarei*, or kneeling bow (*see photos at end of chapter*). The teacher turns and bows to the school shrine—usually the photos of past masters and the American and Japanese flags. All the students bow with him.

The class then stands and forms a circle, and all *rei*, or standing bow (*see photos at end of chapter*), to each other.

The actual class begins with a series of warm-up exercises. These are push-ups, sit-ups, jumping-jacks, stretching exercises, and the like. After warming up, the class begins to practice basics. One master said, "True karate is nothing but the practice of sound basic techniques." Basics are stances, weight shifting, punches, strikes, kicks, and blocks. While there are many styles of karate, each has its own set of basic techniques. From there the class begins to concentrate on either self-defense techniques, *kata* (formal exercises), or *kumite* (free-fighting).

Q. *What are kata?*

A. Kata, or formal exercises, are the essence of karate practice. True karate is the continual practice of kata. They are the heart and the root of all the basic moves and principles of any karate system. Most of the kata practiced today—there are as many as 50 in some karate systems—were created centuries ago by the Chinese and later changed to suit the lifestyles of the Okinawans and Japanese.

Kata are organized sets of techniques performed in a special sequence alone against imaginary opponents. Kata are practiced either in a group or by yourself so you can concentrate on developing the proper speed and timing.

Many people think that karate is only free-fighting, like the full-contact karate fights you see on ESPN (cable TV). Yet there was a time in history when free-fighting was not allowed and the only way to practice karate was through the kata. Therefore, today the kata are the primary teaching device used by karate teachers all over the world.

Most kata begin and end in the same spot. Some have only 15 moves, while others have more than 100. They take from 30 seconds to over two minutes to perform at their correct speed.

All kata are very difficult to perfect. Thus, a 15-move kata that takes 30 seconds to do may take 20 years to do *correctly*. Because of this difficulty, which forges a fighting spirit, kata training has always been very important to karate. Without this fighting spirit, you cannot succeed in karate.

Q. *What is free-fighting?*

A. Free-fighting is the application of the basic techniques and the moves learned through the kata. Free-fighting is often the most exciting part of karate for both students and spectators. This is where your skill will be put to the test because instead of punching and kicking at the air (as in kata) you will be facing a walking, breathing, moving opponent—one that strikes back. Although there are set rules to prevent injury to the practitioners, in reality just about anything goes in free-fighting. Thus the term *free*-fighting.

During free-fighting, students apply all they have learned. This gives them the chance to discover what techniques work for them and which do not.

The concept of free-fighting (*jiyu-kumite*, in Japanese) is really quite new. It was developed by Master Goden Yamaguchi of the *goju-ryu* style of karate in the 1930s. The idea was to focus a *killing* blow just short (usually one to two inches) of making fatal contact. The key phrase in those days was *perfect control*. A mistake could permanently injure an opponent.

Today, thanks to organized rules and mandatory safety equipment, free-fighting, or *sport karate*, is a fun and challenging game played each weekend by literally thousands of people.

Q. *Why are there so many styles of karate?*

A. There are really only a handful of legitimate karate styles. The main ones are the *shotokan* style (the founding style of karate), the *goju-ryu* (hard/soft) style, the *shito-ryu*, *wado-ryu* (karate/ju-jutsu style), and the *kyokushinkai-kan* system of Mas Oyama. These are the largest of the karate styles in Japan. In Okinawa the main systems are *shorin-ryu* and *goju-ryu*.

Each of these styles has its own set of kata that can be traced to antiquity. However, there are really more similarities than differences. Each style aims at disciplining its practitioners, with fighting being the least important of its aims. Remember, although there are many systems, their end goals are the same, making them all a part of the whole of karate.

THE BOW

The Standing Bow
Japanese: *Rei*

Stand erect with your hands at your sides and your feet together (*photo 2-1*). Bow from the waist, keeping your head up (*photo 2-2*). For a variation used in some schools, bow with hands folded at mid-chest level (*photo 2-3*).

2-1   2-2   2-3

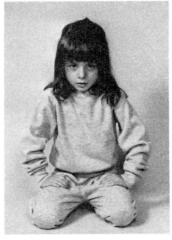

2-4   2-5

The Kneeling Bow
Japanese: *Za-rei*

The kneeling bow is the ultimate sign of respect and is used before and after each karate class. Begin bow in the kneeling position with hands resting on thighs (*photo 2-4*). Bow from the waist, lowering the head and placing hands on the floor (*photo 2-5*).

REMEMBER

Night after night . . . in the courtyard of the Azato house as the master looked on, I would practice kata . . . time and again, week after week, sometimes month after month, until I had mastered it to my teacher's satisfaction. This constant repetition of a single kata was grueling, often exasperating, and on occasion humiliating. . . . But practice was strict, and I was never permitted to move on to another kata until Azato was convinced that I had satisfactorily understood the one I had been working on.

Master Gichin Funakoshi
Father of Modern Karate
from Karate-do: My Way of Life

3

WARM-UPS AND STRETCHING, STANCES AND SHIFTING

Karate training is a very well-rounded means of gaining physical fitness and self-confidence. It is, however, strenuous, so you must prepare your body for it.

You cannot put your key in a car and drive it off immediately. In order for the car to work effectively and without damage to the engine, it is best to give the car a few minutes to warm up. Your body is pretty much the same. To get the most out of it, give it about 10 minutes of warm-up before heavy training.

WARM-UPS AND STRETCHING

Karate warm-up/stretching exercises are designed to loosen up the muscles and joints. These are the parts of the body that are most often injured in karate due to inadequate warm-up time.

A few things to keep in mind are: never stretch to the point of tearing a muscle; never strain during warm-up; and always breathe properly while stretching. Let's take one at a time.

When you are stretching it is important to keep the body and muscles relaxed. Do not try to go beyond what your body is capable of. If you do,

you take the chance of tearing a muscle.

Never strain or tighten the muscles when stretching and warming up. Stay relaxed. A relaxed body is able to stretch better and warm up more effectively.

Last, always breathe correctly when stretching. If you breathe incorrectly, you take the chance of developing lung and heart conditions. The golden rule is: the time to inhale is when your body is under the least amount of stress, and the time to exhale is when your body is performing a strenuous movement.

Exercise 1: Neck Rotations

Flexibility in the neck is very important to the karateka. Being able to move your neck freely makes you more coordinated and more alert. Begin the exercise either standing or kneeling. First, simply roll your head around clockwise and then counterclockwise (*photos 3-1 to 3-4*). Do this for about 30 seconds. The circling movements should be slow and smooth. Next, switch tempo and look to the left (*photo 3-5*) and then to the right (*photo 3-6*) briskly and sharply. Do this about 10 times.

3-1

3-2

3-3

3-4

3-5

3-6

3-7   3-8   3-9   3-10

Exercise 2: Arm Circles

This exercise warms up the shoulder for punching and striking techniques. Begin by crossing the arms at waist level (*photo 3-7*). Circle them upward, bringing the arms above the head (*photo 3-8*). At this point the hands separate as you bring them down (*photo 3-9*) to end at start position (*photo 3-10*). This motion should be made briskly as if your arms were the propellers on a helicopter.

Exercise 3: Squat Stretches

Begin by squatting down—as if sitting on top of a horse (*photo 3-11*). Resting your hands on your upper thighs, squat downward, keeping one leg straight while bending the support leg (*photo 3-12*). Hold position for a few seconds and then switch to opposite leg (*photo 3-13*). Alternate one leg at a time for about one minute. For best results, be sure to keep the supporting leg's foot on the ground. *Do not* go up on the ball of the foot.

Exercise 4: Leg Exercises I

1. The first movement is to extend one leg while sitting on the floor, at the same time tucking the other leg neatly into the thigh (*photo 3-14*). Keeping the straight leg locked, lower the head to the knee, stretching the muscles in the back of the thigh and lower back (*photo 3-15*). Repeat with other leg.

2. For the second movement, continue sitting, this time opening the legs as far as is comfortable (*photo 3-16*). Grasp the right leg and lower the head to the knee (*photo 3-17*). After holding this position for several seconds, switch and do the same on the left side (*photo 3-18*).

3-11

3-12

3-13

3-14

3-16

3-15

3-17

3-18

3-19

3-20

3-21

3-22

Exercise 5: Leg Exercises II

1. Begin the first movement by sitting on the ground with both legs together and stretched out in front of you (*photo 3-19*). *Keeping the back straight*, lower the head to rest on both knees (*photo 3-20*).

2. The second movement begins by rolling onto your back, keeping both legs extended and together (*photo 3-21*). Grasping your legs behind the knees, lower your legs to your head (*photo 3-22*). As in step 1 of this exercise, be sure to keep the legs *straight*.

Exercise 6: Leg Exercises III

In this two-person exercise the leg is stretched to develop good kicking action. Begin by having your partner squat down; place your foot on his shoulder. Keeping the leg straight and the knee

3-23

3-24

3-25

3-26

3-27

pointed to the side (the knee should *never* be facing up), have your partner begin to stand up, rising as far as he can without making the stretching action uncomfortable for you (*photo 3-23*). Hold the position for several minutes. *Note:* Be sure to lean forward—into the stretch—rather than backward away from the stretch.

Exercise 7: Butterfly Stretch

Placing the soles of both feet together, draw feet in toward groin as close as is comfortable (*photo 3-24*). Keeping a tight grip on the feet, lower the top half of body to the floor (*photo 3-25*). *Note:* Be sure to keep the back straight when lowering body forward.

Exercise 8: Back Stretching

Stand back to back with your partner and lock your arms together (*photo 3-26*). Keeping your backs pressed tightly together, bend down on your knees, at the same time leaning forward and lifting partner off the floor. To lift partner higher, straighten your legs (*photo 3-27*).

The object of the stretch is to *relax* when you're the one being lifted so your back is arched and stretched. If you are the lifter, you must remain tight (muscle-tensed) and aware so as to not drop your partner. Both you and your partner should alternate on the lifting action for several minutes. Each lifting action should be held for several seconds.

3-28

3-29

3-30

STANCES AND SHIFTING OF WEIGHT

Stances are postures the body takes in order to deliver a particular technique. Stances are the most effective method for keeping your balance. You should practice them often so the body gets comfortable with them and they begin to feel natural.

Closed Stance
Japanese: *Heisoku-dachi*

This stance is used when you are about to begin a movement and after you have finished a movement. Simply stand with both feet together with weight equally distributed on them (*photo 3-28*).

Open-Toe Stance
Japanese: *Musubi-dachi*

This stance is an alternative to the closed stance, with toes pointed out (*photo 3-29*).

Open Stance
Japanese: *Hachiji-dachi*

This stance may be the most natural and comfortable of all the stances. Place the feet so that the heels are separated by a distance roughly equal to the width of the hips and point the toes outward at a 45-degree angle. Weight is distributed equally on both feet (*photo 3-30*).

Horse Stance
Japanese: *Kiba-dachi*

Bend the knees, keep the upper body straight, and look straight ahead (*photo 3-31*). The stance resembles the position for riding a horse, which is why it is called the *horse stance*. Try as well as you can to keep the toes pointed ahead (how well you can do this depends on your body type and bone structure).

Square Stance
Japanese: *Shiko-dachi*

This stance is the same as the Horse Stance except that the feet are turned outward at an angle of 45 degrees and the hips are closer to the floor (*photo 3-32*).

Front (or Forward) Stance
Japanese: *Zen-kutsu-dachi*

Lower the hips and bend the front knee so that it is over the front foot (*photo 3-33*). (*See photo 3-34 for close-up detail.*) Keep the back leg straight with the upper body held upright and facing straight ahead. Sixty percent of body weight is on the front foot with 40 percent on the rear leg.

3-31

3-32

3-33

3-34

3-35

3-36

3-37

3-38

3-39

3-40

Back Stance
Japanese: *Kokutsu-dachi*

With feet spread slightly farther apart than shoulder width, lower the hips (by slightly bending the knees) and place 60 percent of the weight on the rear leg and 40 percent on the front leg (*photo 3-35*). This stance is very strong to the rear and is excellent for blocking.

T Position
Japanese: *Teiji-dachi*

The feet in this stance form a *T*, with the back foot the top of the *T* and the front foot the base of the *T* (*photo 3-36*). The feet are only about six inches apart with weight distributed equally.

Cat Stance
Japanese: *Neko-ashi-dachi*

To assume a Cat Stance, begin with a Back Stance (above) and withdraw the front foot until the heel is raised and 10 percent of body's weight rests on the ball of the foot (*photo 3-37*). This is a light/fast stance for quick movements.

Hourglass Stance
Japanese: *Sanchin-dachi*

For this stance the right foot is behind the left with toes and knees turned inward (*photo 3-38*). You can easily move into any other stance from this one, which is a very stable and popular position.

X Stance
Japanese: *Juji-dachi*

To assume this stance, start with a Back Stance (above) and draw the rear foot forward. Bend the knees slightly and support 10 percent of body's weight on the ball of the rear foot (*photo 3-39*).

Crane Stance
Japanese: *Tsuru-ashi-dachi*

This stance is assumed by drawing one foot off the ground and holding it near the knee of the supporting leg. Slightly bend the knee of the support leg (*photo 3-40*).

3-41   3-42   3-43

3-44   3-45   3-46

Shifting

Every stance above is a base for the delivery of a particular technique. This base must be very *stable*. Therefore, in order to move about—in order to stay with a moving opponent—you must be able to shift your weight from stance to stance to cover a large distance.

Single-Leg-Stance Shifting

This is shifting from one stance to another by moving only one leg. The reasoning behind this is to use one stance to block and then shift weight forward into a stronger stance for punching. Example:

1. Start from a Cat Stance (*photo 3-41*).
2. The rear leg does *not* move. Slide the front leg forward across the floor (*photo 3-42*).
3. This puts you in a Front Stance (*photo 3-43*). From this position a powerful strike can be delivered.

Crossover Stepping

This is an excellent way to move up and back. Just about any stance can use the Crossover Stepping method.

1. Begin by assuming a particular stance; in this case we have used the Horse Stance (*photo 3-44*).
2. Use the right leg to step over the left leg (the stepover stance is an X Stance position) (*photo 3-45*).
3. Draw the left foot out, forming another Horse Stance (*photo 3-46*).

3-47   3-48   3-49

3-50   3-51   3-52

Forward Circle Stepping

This stepping technique is the one used most often in karate. It is used to step forward (or backward if you reverse the direction). When stepping forward you commit your body weight to a lunging action, which adds great power to techniques.

1. Begin by assuming a Front Stance (*photo 3-47*).

2. Draw the rear leg forward so that it rests near the front foot (*photo 3-48*).

3. Continue the forward stepping action, making the stepping leg form an arch until it assumes another Front Stance position (*photo 3-49*).

Straight Forward Stepping

This stepping action is used to step forward (or backward if you reverse the action). It differs from the Forward Circle Stepping because instead of arching the step when you step forward you simply step straight ahead. This stepping

3-53

3-54

action is used most often with a Back Stance.

1. Assume a Back Stance (*photo 3-50*).

2. Step forward by bringing the rear foot to the front foot (*photo 3-51*).

3. Continue the action by thrusting the stepping foot straight ahead, forming a Back Stance in the opposite direction (*photo 3-52*).

Hip Shifting

This method of weight shifting is a powerful jerking action of the *hips only*. The legs do not step forward or backward. This shifting is used during punching or kicking actions when you want to add that extra power by putting your body behind the technique. To illustrate the body movement, the karateka in the photo is holding a pole. By watching the pole, you can see the movement that is involved.

1. Begin from a Back Stance (*photo 3-53*).

2. Shift the body weight forward, twisting the

right hip to form a front stance (*photo 3-54*). This twisting of the hip is the secret to karate's punching power.

Tips on Stance Training

1. Remember that the key to proper karate techniques is a strong foundation. This foundation is the stance. Because of this, you should practice the stances many times a day until they begin to feel natural.

2. Use a mirror when practicing the stances so you can compare your movements with the ones in the photos.

3. Try using karate shifting techniques in everyday life. When you are walking down a crowded corridor at school, try stance shifting to avoid bumping your classmates. You can also try to get from one end of the hall to the other without bumping another person and using only one particular shifting method.

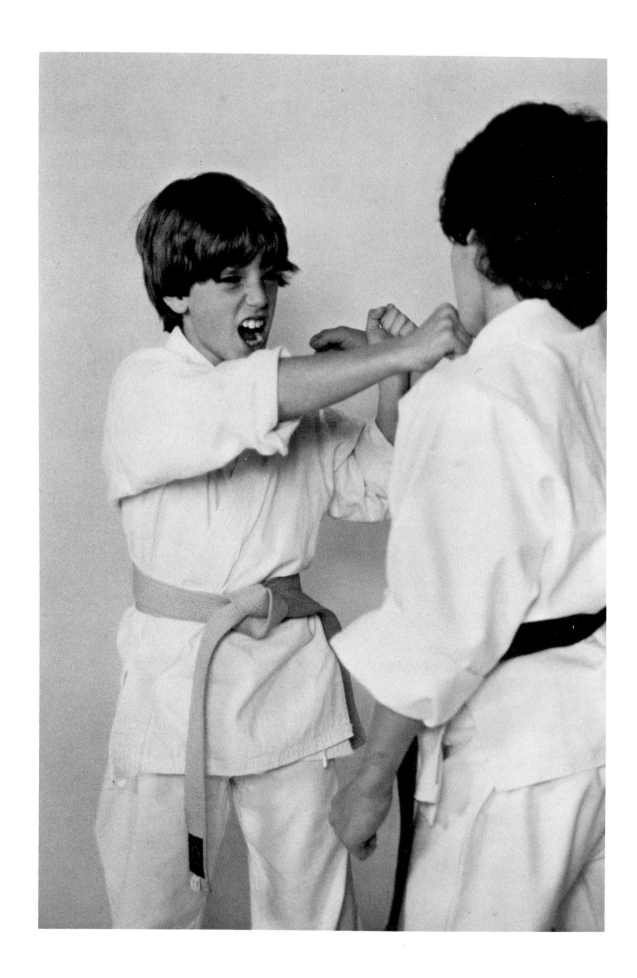

PART II
A PRIMER ON BASICS

USING YOUR HANDS EFFECTIVELY

Using your hands effectively involves learning how to form correct hand weapons, learning to deliver powerful punching and striking techniques, and learning how to block.

When reading this chapter, remember that all punching, blocking, and striking techniques require a strong stance. Therefore, do not move ahead to this chapter until you have learned and mastered the ability to stand—karate style!

FORMING HAND WEAPONS

Forming a fist
Japanese: *Seiken*

1. Begin by holding the hand open (*photo 4-1*).
2. Curl the fingers, forming a very *tight* fist (*photo 4-2*).
3. Form the fist by placing the thumb on the outside of the hand, keeping the index finger tight (*photo 4-3*). Striking surface is made up of the index and middle knuckles.
4. A variation on forming the fist is to keep the index finger loose and wrap the thumb around the index finger for support (*photo 4-4*). The reason some people do it this way is to form a flat striking surface on the top of the fist.

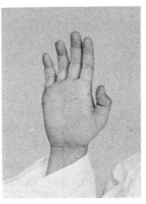

4-1

4-2

4-3

4-4

25

Knife Hand
Japanese: *Shuto*

The knife hand is the famous "karate chop." The striking surface is the edge of the hand.

1. Straighten the fingers and hold them close together.

2. Bend the tips of the fingers, which tenses the edge of palm.

3. Tuck the thumb neatly above the knuckle of the index finger (*photo 4-5*).

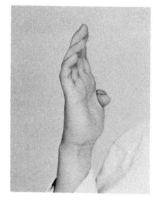 

4-5   4-6

Ridge Hand
Japanese: *Haito*

The Ridge Hand is the opposite of the Knife Hand. Striking surface is the exact opposite of the Knife Hand. Instead of the bottom edge of hand, the top ridge of the hand is used (*photo 4-6*).

4-7

Finger Thrust
Japanese: *Nukite*

Again, the hand is formed exactly the same as for the Knife Hand. This time, however, the striking surface is the fingertips (*photo 4-7*).

Palm Heel
Japanese: *Teisho*

Curl the fingers of the hand back and tuck in the thumb, at the same time bending the wrist to form a solid striking surface with the palm heel of the hand (*photo 4-8*). This is a very powerful technique that causes very little injury to the hand.

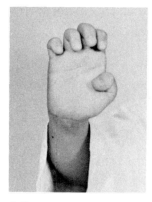 

4-8   4-9

Bent-Wrist Strike
Japanese: *Koken*

Hold all the fingers together and bend the wrist downward to expose the back of the wrist (*photo 4-9*). Striking surface is top of wrist.

Middle-Knuckle Strike
Japanese: *Nakadaka-ken*

Form a regular fist, but this time allow the middle knuckle to stick out. Squeeze the middle finger tightly with the index and ring fingers to hold the knuckle in place during a striking action.

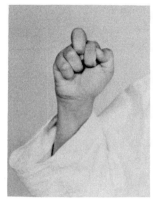

4-10

4-11

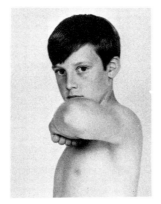

4-12

4-13

(*photo 4-10*). Soft areas of the body (neck, groin, side) are favorite targets for this hand weapon.

Fist Hammer
Japanese: *Tettsui*

After forming a correct fist (*seiken*), use the bottom of the fist (the little finger side) to strike the tarqet (*photo 4-11*). Strikes with this hand weapon are delivered with a snapping action of the forearm.

Elbow
Japanese: *Empi (or Hiji)*

This part of the arm can be used to deliver a powerful blow to any part of an opponent's body (*photo 4-12*). This weapon is particularly effective when your opponent is very close to you.

PUNCHING TECHNIQUES

Straight Punch
Japanese: *Choku-zuki*

The Straight Punch is delivered at a target directly ahead with the hand weapon being a fist (*seiken*).

1. Start from an Open Stance (*heisoku-dachi*) with one fist extended and the punching arm (in this case the right arm) held palm up at side (*photo 4-13*).

2. Begin to twist the fist as you punch in a straight line from the hip position to the target (*photo 4-14*).

3. Turn the forearm 180 degrees inward before you hit the target (*photo 4-15*). By doing so, you will have a more powerful punch.

4-14

4-15

4-16

4-17

4-18

4-19

4-20

4-21

4-22

4-23   4-24   4-25

Application

Facing your opponent (*photo 4-16*), deliver the Straight Punch to his midsection (*photo 4-17*).

Reverse Punch
Japanese: *Gyaku-zuki*

The Reverse Punch is a *very* powerful technique that is delivered from a strong, stable stance—namely, the Front Stance.

1. Begin by assuming a Front Stance with nonpunching arm extended and the punching hand (in this case the right) held at hip with palm up (*photo 4-18*).
2. Follow the same concept in twisting the hand forward as in the Straight Punch (*chokuzuki*) (*photo 4-19*).
3. Upon impact, the fist should twist 180 degrees (*photo 4-20*). The power of the arm as well as the hip (see section on "Hip Shifting," Chapter 3) is used in the punching action.

Tips

1. Keep the hips low so your stance is stable.
2. Do not use the power of the arm alone to deliver the punch, but use these factors along with hip shifting (see Chapter 3).
3. Upon impact with target, push off a little with the rear leg for extra power.

Jab (Obverse Punch)
Japanese: *Kizami-zuki*

The Jab is a lunging type of punch, which means you lunge your weight forward into the punching action for added power.

1. Assume a Back Stance with right leg in rear position and punching hand (in this case the left hand) held at hip with palm up (*photo 4-21*).
2. Execute the jab by twisting the punching hand 180 degrees and shifting the weight forward into a Front Stance (*photo 4-22*). This weight shifting makes the Jab a very powerful and quick punch.

Lunging Punch
Japanese: *Oi-zuki (or Jun-zuki)*

The Lunging Punch is a punching attack that is delivered after a long forward step. The forward momentum of the body gives added power to the Lunging Punch, making it the most powerful punching action in karate.

1. Assume a left Front Stance with left hand held out and punching hand (in this case the right hand) held at hip with palm up (*photo 4-23*).
2. Execute a Forward Circle Step (see Chapter 3) (*photo 4-24*).
3. On the completion of the Forward Circle Step, execute a Straight Punch (*photo 4-25*).

4-26   4-27

4-28

Vertical Fist Punch
Japanese: *Tate-zuki*

1. Assume a Front Stance with punching hand (in this case the right hand) held at side with palm facing body (*photo 4-26*).

2. Strike forward with the right fist, using hip twisting for added power (*photo 4-27*).

Application

Facing opponent (*photo 4-28*), deliver the Vertical Fist Punch to his midsection (*photo 4-29*). The target areas for this punch are usually the face, the point under the nose, and the middle of the chest.

Close (Upside-Down) Punch
Japanese: *Ura-zuki*

1. Assume a T Stance with an on-guard hand position with both hands raised to protect the face (*photo 4-30*).

2. Shift your weight forward, forming a Front Stance while you begin to twist the fist (*photo 4-31*).

3. Continue to twist the fist until the inside of the wrist faces up (*photo 4-32*).

4-29

Application

Facing opponent in ready stance with both hands raised to protect the face (*photo 4-33*), deliver the Close Punch to his solar plexus (middle of chest) (*photo 4-34*). Remember to flex the muscles of the back and side at the moment of impact; otherwise the Close Punch will be weak. Favorite target areas are the face, midsection, and side of body.

4-30

4-31

4-32

4-33

4-34

4-35

4-36

4-37

Cross Punch (or Twisting Punch)
Japanese: *Juji-zuki*

Like the Lunging Punch, this is a very powerful punch, but it can be used when you are close to your opponent (the Lunging Punch is used when you are at some distance from your opponent).

1. Assume a Closed Stance (Open Stance is an alternative), with the nonpunching hand in a blocking position and the punching hand (in this case the right hand) held at hip with palm up (*photo 4-35*).

2. Punch with the right fist, twisting the body counterclockwise while forming an X Stance with feet (*photo 4-36*).

Application

You are facing your opponent, who has just punched at you, and you have just blocked that punch (*photo 4-37*). Deliver a Cross Punch to his chin (*photo 4-38*). To get the most power from the punch, be sure to jerk the hip into the punching action.

4-38

4-39

4-40

4-41

STRIKING TECHNIQUES

Knife-Hand Strike (from outside inward)
Japanese: *Uchi-shuto-uchi*

1. Assume a left Front Stance (left foot forward) while holding the striking hand (in this case the right hand) behind the right ear, forming a Knife Hand (*photo 4-39*).

2. Twist the hips into the striking action as you snap the right hand forward, hitting with the edge of the palm (*photo 4-40*).

Application

Face your opponent with your striking hand held high (*photo 4-41*). Twist your body into the striking action as you strike your opponent on the side of the neck (*photo 4-42*). Remember to stretch the hand until the palm is flat and press the fingers together. Keep the wrist firm to ensure a strong snapping action. Relax the elbow to provide speed in the striking action.

4-42

4-43

4-44

4-45

4-46

Knife-Hand Strike (from inside outward) Japanese: *Soto-shuto-uchi*

1. Assume a right Front Stance (right foot forward), while holding the striking hand (in this case the right hand) behind the left ear (*photo 4-43*).

2. Lean into the striking action as you draw the right hand down in a backhanded action (*photo 4-44*). This is a very powerful striking action that is used many times in board-breaking demonstrations.

Application

Face your opponent as you draw your striking hand across your chest to rest under your left ear (*photo 4-45*). Draw the striking hand down to the side of opponent's neck (*photo 4-46*).

4-47

4-48

4-49

Descending Palm Heel Strike
Japanese: *Omote teisho-uchi*

This is a fast Palm Heel Strike aimed at opponent's groin. The same hand that blocks is used to deliver the strike as you use a quick hip-jerking action for added power.

1. For practice purposes, begin technique from a Front Stance (right foot forward) with both hands in palm heel position at hips with palms up (*photo 4-47*).

2. Snap a stance change. That is, snap from a right Front Stance facing forward to a right Back Stance facing rear. At the same time, deliver a downward palm heel thrust to groin area (*photo 4-48*).

Application

Face your opponent, who has attempted to strike you. Block the strike with your right hand as you form a right Cat Stance (*photo 4-49*). Shift weight to form a left Cat Stance, at the same time lowering your right hand and delivering a Palm Heel Strike to opponent's groin (*photo 4-50*).

4-50

4-51   4-52   4-53

BLOCKING TECHNIQUES

Rising Block
Japanese: *Age-uke*

1. Face your opponent (left in photos) (*photo 4-51*).

2. As your attacker punches, move the blocking arm from its start position upward and forward until it contacts the opponent's arm (*photo 4-52*). At the moment of contact, bring your forearm back toward your head, ending in a position directly in front of your forehead. In its complete course, the blocking arm describes a curve.

3. Repeat same procedure on opposite side (*photo 4-53*).

Outside-Inward Block
Japanese: *Soto-uke*

1. Face your opponent (left in photos) in a ready position (*photo 4-54*).

2. As your opponent punches with his right hand, raise your left arm to the side with the fist near the left side (*photo 4-55*). Drive the arm downward and forward and block the opponent's punch to your body.

3. Repeat same procedure on right side (*photo 4-56*).

Inside-Outward Block
Japanese: *Uchi-uke*

1. Face your opponent (left in photos) and assume a start position (*photo 4-57*).

2. Opponent attempts to punch you with his right hand. Place the left fist in front of face with arm in line with the right hip and with the back of the fist facing forward. Bring the forearm up and forward, using the elbow as a pivot. Deflect the opponent's body attack by striking his forearm to the side with the top of your wrist from the inside outward (*photo 4-58*).

3. Repeat same procedure on opposite side (*photo 4-59*).

4-54

4-55

4-56

4-57

4-58

4-59

4-60

4-61

Downward Block
Japanese: *Gedan-barai*

1. Face opponent (left in photos) and assume a ready posture (*photo 4-60*).

2. Opponent attempts to punch you in the groin with his left hand (*photo 4-61*). Start the Downward Block with the left fist beside the right ear. Aim the back of the fist outward to the side. Strike downward, straightening the elbow, then deflect the opponent's attack to the side with the bottom of your wrist.

3. Repeat same procedure on opposite side (*photo 4-62*).

TIPS ON USING YOUR HANDS EFFECTIVELY

1. To deliver a *very* powerful karate punch, stretch the arm smoothly and rapidly toward the target. Release all unnecessary tension from the arm and hand at the start, but be sure to concentrate all the power of the body in the punching fist at the moment of impact.

2. True power in hand techniques can be concentrated only when the hips, chest, shoulders, arms, wrists, and fists are firmly linked and all necessary muscles function fully.

4-62

3. In blocking, forearm rotation and timing are closely related. Obviously, the block must not be applied too early or too late. Judge the opponent's intent and assume the starting position of your block, but be sure to allow enough time to parry or deflect the attack.

5

THOSE FABULOUS KARATE KICKS

Without a doubt, kicking techniques, when properly applied, have a more powerful effect on an opponent than attacks with the hands. However, mastering kicking techniques requires much time and effort.

Good balance is essential to kicking because the body weight rests on one leg, called the *support leg.* And it's even more difficult to keep your balance when the kicking foot hits the target because of the strong backlash of the kick.

To counteract this shock, place the supporting foot firmly on the ground and fully tighten the ankle of the supporting leg. Attempt to absorb the shock with the ankle, knee, and hip of the supporting leg and keep the upper body well balanced and as straight as possible.

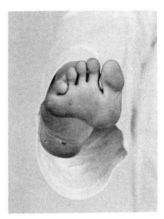

5-1

ball of the foot, it is possible to deliver kicks to opponent's face, chest, abdomen, and groin.

FOOT WEAPONS

Ball of the Foot
Japanese: *Koshi*

Many types of kicks use the ball of the foot as the foot weapon, especially the front kick (*photo 5-1*). By curling the toes upward and using the

Foot Edge and the Heel
Japanese: *Sokuto* and *Kakato,* respectively

This is a very popular foot weapon used in Reverse Crescent Kicks and Side Kicks. The edge of the foot on the side of the little toe serves as the striking area (*photo 5-2*). Toes can be curled

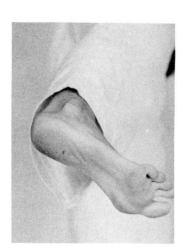

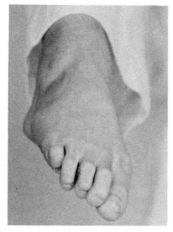

5-2

5-3

either up (modern way) or down (ancient way) to expose this striking surface.

Also, the heel is an excellent and strong foot weapon when delivering power kicks like the Back Kick. Form the foot in the same way as the edge of the foot, but use the heel as the striking surface.

Instep
Japanese: *Haisoku*

This is the top of the foot from the toes to the ankle. The foot is stretched downward and the toes pointed downward (*photo 5-3*).

KICKING METHODS
Front Kick
Japanese: *Mae-geri*

From a Front Stance, this kick can be done from both the front leg and the rear leg. Rear-leg kicks are more powerful, while front leg kicks are usually faster.

1. Begin from start position (*photo 5-4*).
2. Bring the front leg up to a chamber position (*photo 5-5*). *Chamber position* refers to the act of bringing the kicking foot up to the knee of the supporting leg.
3. Pointing the knee and the toes at the target, relax the knee and extend the kicking leg in a *straight* line to the target, using the ball of the foot as the kicking weapon (*photo 5-6*).
4. Return leg to chamber position (*photo 5-7*).
5. Lower kicking leg to floor and reassume start position (*photo 5-8*).

Application

Face your opponent (left in photos) (*photo 5-9*). He attempts to punch at your face. Immediately bring your rear leg into chamber position (*photo 5-10*) and deliver a Front Kick to opponent's groin (*photo 5-11*). Bring your leg back to chamber position (*photo 5-12*) and assume a strong fighting stance in the event your opponent continues to attack (*photo 5-13*).

5-4   5-5   5-6   5-7   5-8

5-9

5-10

5-11

5-12

5-13

5-14   5-15   5-16

5-17   5-18

Cutting Kick
Japanese: *Fumikiri*

The Cutting Kick is a kind of side kick. It is used to attack the opponent's leg or instep. The Cutting Kick is effective when the opponent is in front of you or behind you. You simply change the direction of the kick, depending on where the target is.

1. Assume a start position (*photo 5-14*).
2. Bring the kicking leg up to the knee of the support leg (chamber position) (*photo 5-15*).
3. Thrust your foot downward to the side and kick target with the edge of foot. Imagine that your foot is a cleaver or an ax head, cutting into the target (*photo 5-16*).
4. Return to chamber position (*photo 5-17*).
5. Return to start position (*photo 5-18*).

Application

Face your opponent (left in photos) (*photo 5-19*). Turn your side to the opponent and quickly chamber your leg (*photo 5-20*). Execute the Cutting Kick (*photo 5-21*), which knocks opponent to the floor as you rechamber (*photo 5-22*) and assume a fight stance (*photo 5-23*) for follow-up hand attacks.

5-19

5-20

5-21

5-22

5-23

5-24

5-25

5-26

5-27

Side Thrust Kick
Japanese: *Yoko geri-kekomi*

The Side Thrust Kick is a very powerful kicking action that uses the edge of the foot as the striking weapon. Use this kick to attack the solar plexus, chest, or side.

1. Assume a ready position (*photo 5-24*).

2. Shift your weight to the left leg and raise the right leg into chamber position (*photo 5-25*).

3. Kick out to the side, turning the hip so the buttocks face up (*photo 5-26*). Lock the leg on the extension of the kick for a brief second.

4. Return to chamber position and assume a ready stance (*photo 5-27*).

Application

Face your opponent (left in photos) (*photo 5-28*). Opponent attempts to strike your face with the back of his lead hand. Bring your leg into chamber position (*photo 5-29*), grasp the attacking hand, and deliver a Side Thrust Kick (*photo 5-30*) to opponent's side. Immediately return to chamber position (*photo 5-31*) and move into a ready stance (*photo 5-32*) to continue to defend yourself if necessary.

5-28

5-29

5-30

5-31

5-32

5-33   5-34

Back Kick
Japanese: *Ushiro-geri*

The Back Kick is directed against a target to the rear with the heel of the foot as the foot weapon. The kick is delivered with a powerful thrusting action to the solar plexus, abdomen, groin, thigh, or lower leg. It is also a good follow-up technique or can be used in combination with the Front Kick or Side Kick.

1. Assume a start position (*photo 5-33*). Your target is behind you.

2. Look to the rear, at your target, and lift your leg into the chamber position (*photo 5-34*).

3. Lean the body slightly forward and in the same motion straighten your knee and thrust your leg directly behind you (*photo 5-35*).

4. Return to chamber position (*photo 5-36*).

5. Assume a ready stance, facing forward (*photo 5-37*).

5-35

5-36

5-37

5-38

5-39

5-40

5-41

Flying Side Kick
Japanese: *Yoko-tobi-geri*

Flying kicks must be performed with a certain boldness. You must leap high in the air and kick the target at the peak of your leap.

1. Stand in a Closed Stance with hands in a guard position to protect the face (*photo 5-38*).

2. Leap high into the air with both feet, drawing the legs up high near the buttocks (*photo 5-39*).

3. While at the peak of the leap, thrust out a Side Kick (see Side Thrust Kick for details on kick) (*photo 5-40*).

4. Return, like a cat, to the floor on both feet in a solid, stable stance (*photo 5-41*).

Application

Face your opponent (left in photos) (*photo 5-42*). Slide your weight forward and begin to raise your lead hand. Raising your lead hand will make your opponent raise his guard because his attention is on your hand (*photo 5-42*). Leap into the air (*photo 5-44*) and deliver a Flying Side Kick to opponent's chest (*photo 5-45*). Return to floor in a stable ready stance to continue to attack or defend (*photo 5-46*).

-42

5-43

5-44

5-45

5-46

5-47   5-48   5-49

5-50   5-51

Flying and Turning Reverse Crescent Kick
Japanese: *Gyaku-mikazuki-tobi-geri*

This is a very impressive kick and one that takes expert timing and skill to do properly.

1. Assume a start position (*photo 5-47*).

2. Draw the rear leg forward into a chamber position as you begin to spin clockwise (*photo 5-48*).

3. Leap into the air and continue to spin in a clockwise direction, making a full circle (*photo 5-49*).

4. At the completion of the spin, strike opponent with the foot edge of the once supporting foot (*photo 5-50*).

5. Return to a stable on-guard position with both hands protecting the face immediately when both feet touch the ground (*photo 5-51*).

Application

Face your opponent (left in photos) (*photo 5-52*). Slide both feet together into a Closed Stance as you fake a punch to opponent's groin. Opponent blocks this punch (*photo 5-53*), which creates an opening at his head. Leap into the air, spinning clockwise (*photo 5-54*) in a full circle while drawing the right foot across your body

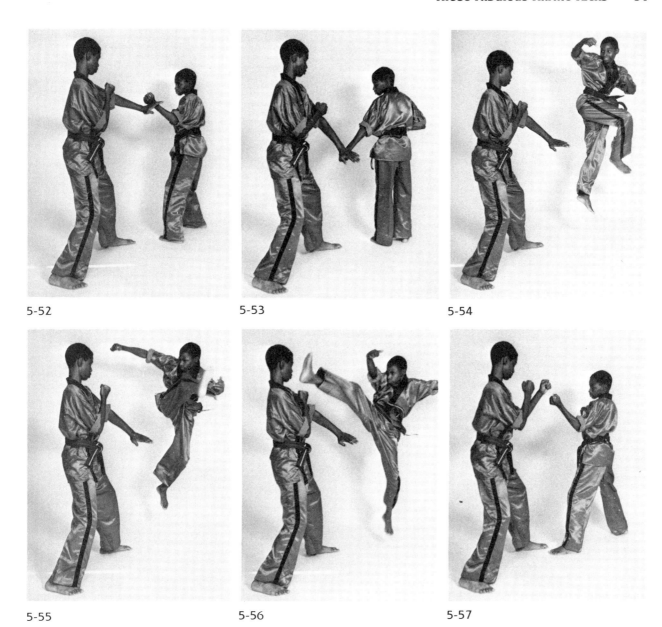

5-52

5-53

5-54

5-55

5-56

5-57

(*photo 5-55*). Deliver your kick in a backhand fashion, striking opponent with the edge of foot (*photo 5-56*). Upon returning to floor, assume a stable ready stance (*photo 5-57*).

TIPS ON DELIVERING MORE EFFECTIVE KICKS

1. When kicking, always keep the entire sole of the supporting foot on the floor. Never raise yourself on the ball of the foot.

2. Always bend the knee of the supporting foot slightly and flex the ankle and knee joints.

3. Concentrate all your power on your foot weapon on the instant of impact with the target. At the same time, thrust the hips into the direction of the kick.

4. Lean the upper body in the direction of the kick. If you lean away from the kick, you will lose your balance (the only exception to this rule is the Back Kick).

5. Always rechamber a kick. Never kick and place the leg on the ground without going to chamber position first.

6. To gain more power in your kicking action, always think of your foot weapon going *through* the target rather than just hitting the surface.

PART III
KATA—KARATE
FORMAL EXERCISES

6

GANKAKU KATA
(CRANE ON A ROCK FORM)

Kata, or the formal exercises of karate, are the essence of karate practice. They are the heart and the root of all basic moves and principles of any karate system. Most of the kata practiced today were invented hundreds of years ago and contain the secrets of karate as the past masters saw it.

Kata are organized sets of techniques performed in a very special sequence alone against an imaginary opponent. These sequences *cannot* change. They must be practiced *exactly* as the masters taught them or they lose their value. Kata movements are battle-tested. The masters used these techniques in life and death situations. Therefore, the kata, as they have been passed down to us, work! They are time-honored and time-proven techniques.

All kata are very difficult to perform, regardless of how easy they may appear at first. A 15-move kata may take 20 years of daily practice to perfect to the highest standard.

There are several key points to remember when doing a kata:

1. Bow before and at the end of each kata.
2. When properly executed, each kata will begin and end at the same spot.

3. Each kata has at least three points during which one *kiais* (shouts).
4. Most kata repeat moves first on the left side and then on the right.
5. Each kata has a spirit. That is, each kata teaches something very special and that something special is the spirit of the kata.

The kata presented in this chapter is called *gankaku.* It means "crane on a rock" form. It comes from the shotokan style of karate. The spirit of the kata is found in its imitations of the movements of the crane. The one-legged stance (*tsuru-ashi-dachi*) is seen in the kata. It represents the crane standing on a rock with only one leg (a pose a crane often takes).

This kata was made popular in the recent movie *The Karate Kid,* when the star of the story was seen practicing on posts on a beach, learning how to keep his balance as well as kick. In the movie, it is the Front Kick, as taught in the *gankaku* kata, that wins the star his most important karate match and thus first place at the tournament.

An important note: Although many of the moves in the kata have been reviewed in the

6-1   6-2   6-3   6-4

preceding chapters on basics, there are just as many that will be new in this presentation. A brief explanation is given; however, we suggest *careful* study of the photos for best understanding.

1. Starting position is an Open Stance with hands at side (*photo 6-1*). BOW!

Note: Moves 2–5 below are done very rapidly, without hesitation.

2. Step back, forming a right Back Stance while placing the right hand over the back of the left hand (*photo 6-2*).

3. With hands crossed, draw them across the body to rest at the left side (*photo 6-3*). This action is a block.

4. Execute a finger Jab (*nukite*) with the right hand (*photo 6-4*).

5. Without hesitation, execute a Knife-Hand Strike (from inside outward) with left hand (*photo 6-5*).

6. Hip shift to left Front Stance and execute a right Reverse Punch (*photo 6-6*). Give a loud shout from the pit of your stomach as you punch. This is called a *kiai*. "Hah!" is common *kiai* sound.

7. Bring right foot to left knee while holding the right arm skyward and the left arm in a horizontal guard position (*photo 6-7*).

8. Pivot clockwise 180 degrees on the left foot and face the rear. Execute a Downward Block (*gedan barai*) with right hand while forming a Horse Stance (*photo 6-8*).

9. Look to the left and form a left Front Stance while crossing both hands to form an X Block (*photo 6-9*).

10. Grasp at the air, pretending to grab someone's lapels, and bring the arms down (*photo 6-10*).

11. Bring your left foot to your right, forming a Cat Stance, at the same time extending both hands to the sides like a crane extending its wings (*photo 6-11*).

12. Pick up your right foot and hold the position for a few seconds like a crane balancing on one leg (*photo 6-12*).

13. Leap into the air (*photo 6-13*), pushing off with the left foot. As the right foot makes contact with the floor, execute a Front Kick with the left leg (*photo 6-14*).

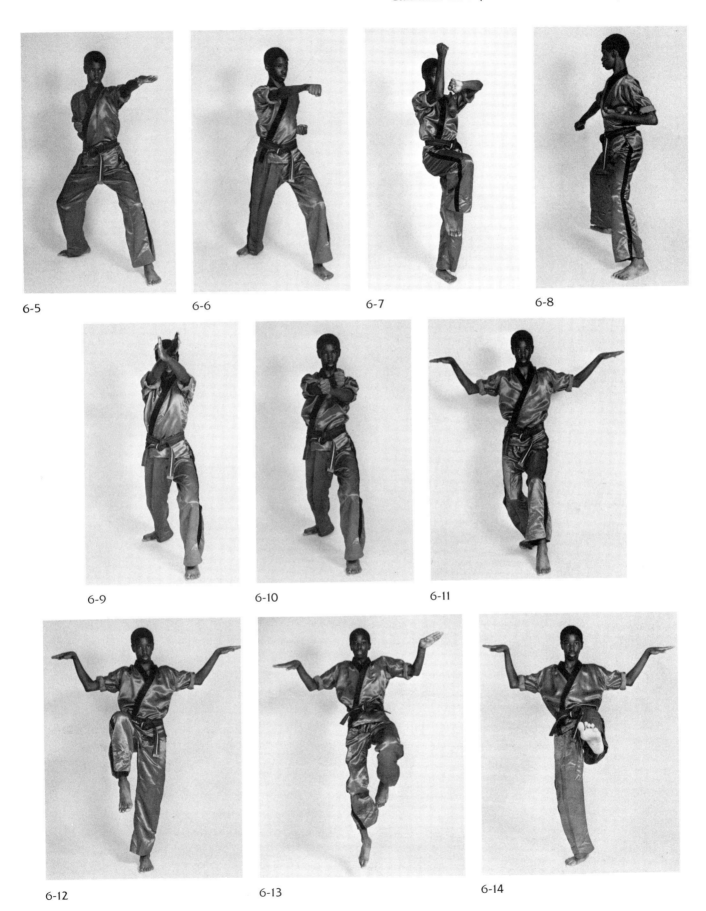

6-5

6-6

6-7

6-8

6-9

6-10

6-11

6-12

6-13

6-14

6-15

6-16

6-17

6-18

14. Lower your left leg to the floor and cross your fists to execute a downward X Block (*photo 6-15*).

15. Look to the rear. Step around to face the rear, forming a left Front Stance and executing another X Block (*photo 6-16*).

16. Look to your rear (forward position at start of kata). Twist yourself clockwise, forming a left Back Stance (there is no stepping in this movement, only a shift of stance). While you shift your stance, execute a downward rear guard position (*photo 6-17*).

17. Step forward, forming a right Back Stance while executing a Downward Block with a left Knife Hand (*photo 6-18*).

18. Step forward, forming a right Front Stance, at the same time executing a Wedging Block. A Wedging Block is a defense against a front choke. To do it, place your hands at face level with forearms crossed and palms facing you

(*photo 6-19*). Twist your arms to the side while turning your palms to face each other (*photo 6-20*). This wedging action is essentially the block. Shout!

19. Look to the left. Twist your body so that you form a Horse Stance toward the left while executing a downward X Block (*photo 6-21*).

20. Bring your arms upward and execute with each an Inside-Outward Block (*photo 6-22*).

21. Cross your arms at head level and pause for a moment (*photo 6-23*). Slowly lower your arms as you slide the legs inward to form an Open Stance (*photo 6-24*).

22. Step to your right side with your right foot, forming a right Back Stance, at the same time raising your right arm and lowering your left arm (*photo 6-25*). (*See photo 6-26 for a side view.*)

23. Step forward with right leg, forming a left Back Stance, while raising the left arm and lowering the right arm (*photo 6-27*).

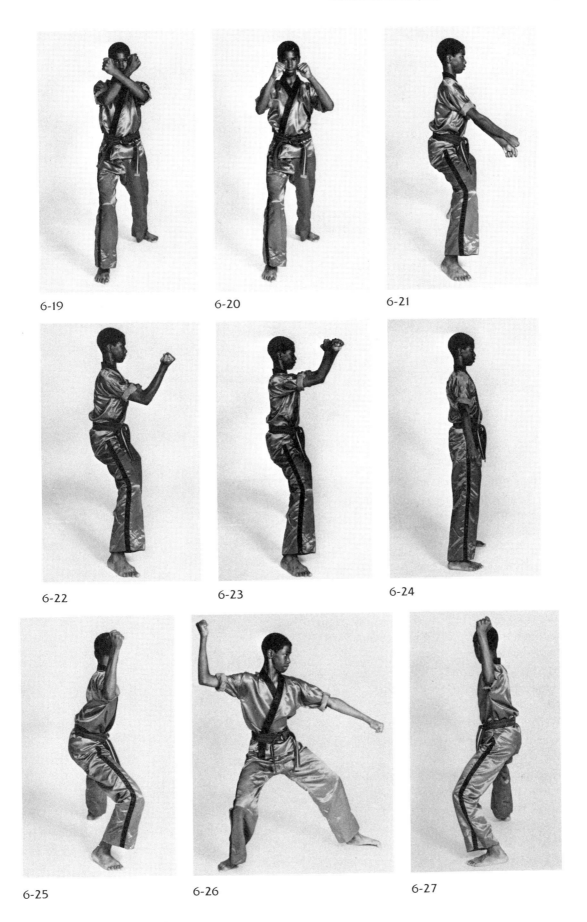

6-19

6-20

6-21

6-22

6-23

6-24

6-25

6-26

6-27

6-28   6-29   6-30

24. Without moving your right leg, draw your left leg to the right, forming an X Stance, while keeping the hands in same position as for movement 23 (*photo 6-28*). Spin your body counterclockwise, forming a right Back Stance, raising the right arm and lowering the left arm (*photo 6-29*). These two moves should be done *very* powerfully with a *snap*.

25. Look to your right while turning your body to the right and dropping down on the right knee. Execute a downward X Block (*photo 6-30*). Shout!

26. Stand up and form a Horse Stance while opening your hands into Knife Hand position (*photo 6-31*).

27. Without changing foot position, execute with each arm an Inside-Outward Block (*photo 6-32*).

28. Raise your hands high above your head, forming the hands into fists (*photo 6-33*). Draw your legs together to form an Open Stance while slowly lowering arms (*photo 6-34*).

29. Place hands on hips with palms facing to your rear and hands forming tight fists (*photo 6-35*).

30. Without actually moving feet from their

6-31   6-32

position, twist your body to the left, going up on the ball of the right foot and blocking an oncoming attack with your right elbow (*photo 6-36*).

31. Repeat movement 30 but to the right (*photo 6-37*).

32. Repeat movement 30 (*photo 6-38*).

6-33

6-34

6-35

6-36

6-37

6-38

6-39   6-40   6-41

33. Twist again to the right, making a three-quarters clockwise circle, at the same time forming an X Stance and executing a double Inside-Outward Block (*photo 6-39*).

34. Looking to the left, raise your left leg to right knee and lock the left instep behind the right knee. Raise your right hand high and bring your left hand low (*photo 6-40*). This stance is the famous "crane on a rock" stance on which the *kata* is based.

35. Unlock your instep from the right knee and bring both hands together at the right side (*photo 6-41*). Execute a left Side Kick (*photo 6-42*).

36. Lower kicking leg to form a right Back Stance, at the same time striking with the back of the left hand (*photo 6-43*).

37. Step forward, forming a right Front Stance, and execute a right Lunging Punch (*photo 6-44*). Shout!

38. Look to the left and raise your left leg to right knee, locking the left instep behind the right knee and raising the right arm and lowering the left arm to form the "crane on a rock" stance (*photo 6-45*).

39. Unlock your instep from the right knee and bring both hands together at right side. Execute a left Side Kick (*photo 6-46*).

40. Lower kicking leg to form a right Back Stance, at the same time striking with the back of the left fist (*photo 6-47*).

41. Without moving feet, Hip Shift to a left Front Stance, at the same time executing a right Reverse Punch (*photo 6-48*).

42. Look to the right. Repeat movement 38 but on the right side (*photo 6-49*).

6-42

6-43

6-44

6-45

6-46

6-47

6-48

6-49

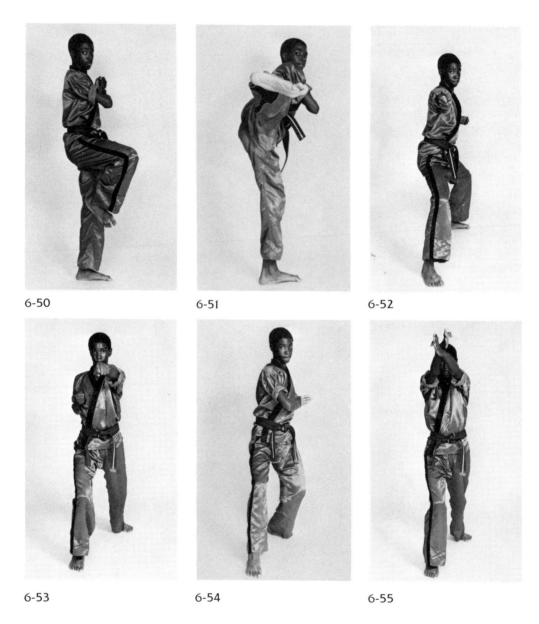

6-50   6-51   6-52

6-53   6-54   6-55

43. Repeat movement 39 but on the right side (*photos 6-50 and 6-51*).

44. Repeat movement 40 on the right side (*photo 6-52*).

45. Repeat movement 41 on the right side (*photo 6-53*).

46. Without moving from position, Hip Shift in reverse to form a left Back Stance while opening fists to Knife Hand position and bringing both hands to left side (*photo 6-54*).

47. Hip Shift forward into a right Front Stance while executing a high X Block (*photo 6-55*).

48. Keep hands in high X Block position and lift the left leg to right knee (*photo 6-56*).

49. Pivot on the right leg 180 degrees and form

a "crane on a rock" stance with left leg locked into position. During this motion, hands remain in high X Block position (*photo 6-57*).

50. Lower hands and execute a left Side Kick (*photo 6-58*).

51. Lower kicking leg to form a right Back Stance while extending the left hand and striking with back of left fist (*photo 6-59*).

52. Step forward into a right Front Stance, executing a right Lunging Punch (*photo 6-60*). Shout!

53. Pivot around 180 degrees to face the forward position at the start of the kata. Raise hands over face in a crossed position (*photo 6-61*).

54. Lower hands slowly to close the *kata* (*photo 6-62*). Bow.

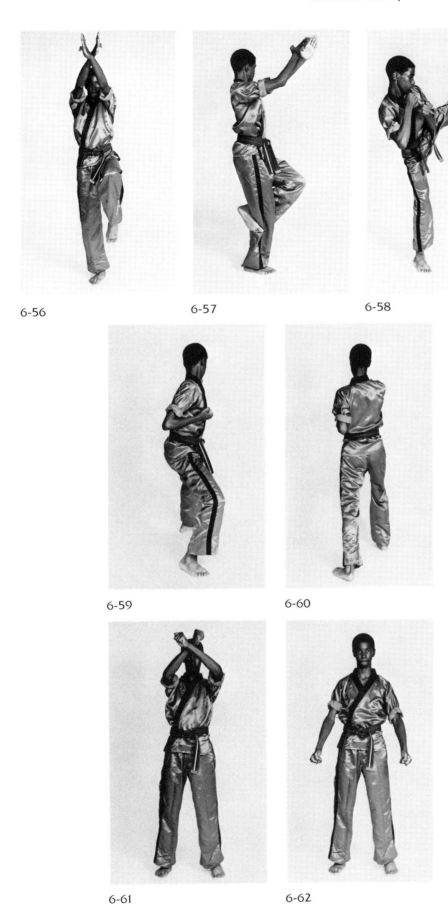

6-56

6-57

6-58

6-59

6-60

6-61

6-62

6-63

6-64

6-65

6-66

SELF-DEFENSE APPLICATIONS OF THE KATA

Application of Moves 2–5

The moves in this part of the kata are intended to be used against someone who has grabbed your wrist.

1. The attacker (right in photos) has grabbed your wrist and is threatening to hurt you (*photo 6-63*).

2. Draw your trapped hand to your right side and step into a Cat Stance (*photo 6-64*).

3. Step back into a Horse Stance, at the same time bringing your trapped hand to your left side and turning the attacker's arm so his elbow faces skyward (*photo 6-65*).

4. While your attacker is temporarily open to attack, deliver a Knife-Hand Strike under his chin (*photo 6-66*).

Application of Move 22

1. Your attacker (right in photos) has just grabbed your wrist and is threatening you with further physical harm (*photo 6-67*).

2. Step back with your right foot into a right Back Stance while bringing your trapped hand upward (*photo 6-68*).

3. Sink yourself into a deep Back Stance, raising your trapped hand to its highest point and delivering a Fist-Hammer Strike to opponent's groin (*photo 6-69*).

6-67

6-68

6-69

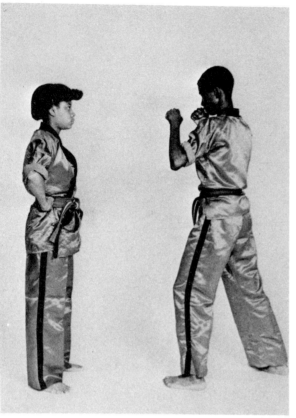

6-70

6-71

Application of Moves 30–32

1. Stand in an Open Stance with both fists resting at your sides. Your opponent (right in photos) is ready to punch you (*photo 6-70*).

2. As opponent punches, twist to the right, blocking the oncoming attack with your elbow (*photo 6-71*).

Application of Moves 38–41

This is the essence of the entire *gankaku* kata. Again, *gankaku* means "crane on a rock." Therefore, the spirit of this kata rests in the application of the "crane on a rock" stance.

1. Your opponent (right in photos) has attempted to punch you with his right fist. You, however, have assumed a "crane on a rock" stance and have pushed his punching arm to the side (*photo 6-72*).

2. Deliver a Side Kick to opponent's leg (*photo 6-73*).

3. Place the kicking leg down, forming a right Back Stance, as you swing the opponent's attack-

ing arm out to the side (*photo 6-74*).

4. Hip Shift into a left Front Stance and strike the opponent in the face with a right Reverse Punch (*photo 6-75*).

TIPS ON STRONGER KATA PERFORMANCE

1. At the beginning, practice your kata in front of a mirror so you can make your moves perfect.

2. Always act as if you are fighting a real opponent when you are doing a kata. Do *not* treat it like a dance. Your kata is a set of time-proven combat techniques. Perform the kata as if your life depended on it.

3. Concentrate on eye contact. Before you pivot to a certain direction, look in that direction, as if you are looking to see if it is safe. This way, people watching you do kata believe in what you are doing.

4. Be sure to give a deep abdominal shout, *kiai*, at the points required in the kata.

5. Eat, breathe, and sleep your kata. Only then will it become an automatic reflex.

6-72

6-73

6-74

6-75

PART IV
PLAYING THE KARATE GAME

KARATE AS FUN:
THE RULES OF THE GAME

Unlike sports such as football, basketball, and tennis, karate is not as yet an organized activity. This is not to say that it does not have a set of rules, for indeed it does.

However, unlike other sports, there are many types and styles of karate, each different in some respect. Therefore, there is not yet a national organization that represents all types of karate. Karate people, therefore, refer to their sport as "unorganized."

Generally, most noncontact karate matches are organized either by national organizations representing particular styles or by the AAU (Amateur Athletic Union). The rules for noncontact fighting differ slightly from organization to organization, though they are basically pretty much the same.

When entering a karate tournament, you have a choice of several divisions:

- Fighting
- Hard Kata
- Soft Kata
- Weapons

Fighting is a controlled application of karate techniques. What happens is that two people bow and then are watched by a referee and four judges (one at each corner of the fighting area). The players are required to deliver punches and kicks at each other *without making excessive contact* that might hurt one another. For safety's sake, the players wear special gloves and foot protectors.

Points are determined by the referee, who consults the judges for their opinions on each point. A point is awarded when one player delivers a controlled kick, punch, or strike that is not blocked by his opponent. The blow must also (1) be controlled enough so it stops just short of touching the other player's body (or else it touches the player without actually hurting him or her) and (2) be delivered with the full intention of power but, again, without making contact. This prevents the match from becoming a game of who tags whom.

Fighting divisions are broken down by sex (male and female), age, belt, or weight classes (lightweight, middleweight, light heavyweight, heavyweight). The exact way a fighting division is arranged is up to the tournament promoter.

The kata division is often broken down by sex, age, belts, whether the kata is *hard* (delivered in powerful straight lines, like the kata in this book) or *soft* (delivered in gentle, soft circles without the snapping power seen in *hard* kata). Further, many tournaments have *master* kata. This division is for black belts of third degree or higher.

Generally, kata is scored in front of a panel, pretty much the way diving or gymnastics is scored. Each panel member (called a judge) scores the kata from 1 to 10. The average score of all the judges makes up the final score.

Recently, with the increased popularity of karate weapons, many tournaments have created special weapons divisions. The weapons division is usually broken down by belt ranks, and men and women usually compete equally. The scoring system is the same as that used in standard kata divisions.

A number of other divisions have also appeared lately at tournaments. Musical kata, for example, is performed to music and the kata is judged not only on technique but also on its relationship to the music selected.

Kata is also sometimes broken down into traditional and creative. *Traditional* is a kata that was invented by a past master, and *creative* is a kata invented by the player.

There are also breaking divisions. In breaking divisions there are two major categories: breaking form and breaking power. In breaking form you are judged on how entertaining and spectacular the break is. In breaking power, you are judged on how much material (boards, bricks, stones, etc.) you can break through.

Finally, we now have full-contact karate matches. In these, the players wear boxing-type gloves and attack each other until one player is knocked out. In the event there is no knockout, the judges and referee make a decision based on which player performed better throughout the match.

In the next chapter we will look at winning combinations from the East Coast Demo Team, a team of highly talented children who mix gymnastics, break dancing, and superior strategy in order to get the point. The East Coast Demo Team (also known as the Spinning Cobras) have won many tournaments throughout the United States and are fast becoming a major force in peewee and junior fighting divisions. They are also noted for both traditional and creative kata.

8

WINNING NONCONTACT FIGHTING COMBINATIONS PRESENTED BY THE EAST COAST DEMO TEAM

SIKIE "THE JET" HOLLIMANN

At age 14, Sikie enjoys working with her feet. Her favorite kicks are the Front Kick and Roundhouse Kick, which she uses with expert skill and timing.

"Karate is good for everyone. It doesn't matter if you are a girl or a guy. If you aren't that strong, you play up your other talents, such as speed and strategy. If you train correctly, anyone can be good at this game."

Favorite Fight Combination

1. Sikie "The Jet" Hollimann faces her opponent (right in photos) (*photo 8-1*).
2. Sikie delivers a rear-leg Front Kick to the opponent's midsection. This draws the opponent's attention down to his stomach area in order to block (with his elbows) the oncoming kick (*photo 8-2*).

3. Sikie has now created an opening at her opponent's head level. Without lowering her right kicking leg, Sikie immediately changes kicks and catches her opponent on the side of the head with a Roundhouse Kick (*photos 8-3 and 8-4*). This combination would give Sikie a full point.

8-1

8-2

8-3

8-4

MELVIN "LEGS" JAMISON

At age 15, Melvin has earned his first-degree (junior) black belt. Melvin is called "Legs" by his peers because of his ability to score with his legs. He is noted for his incredible jump kicks.

"If you want to be good at karate, you have to practice. Karate is a lot more than a game. It has taught me to believe in myself. I now know I can do whatever I set my mind to doing, thanks to karate."

8-5

8-6

8-7

8-8

Favorite Fight Combination

1. Melvin "Legs" Jamison faces his opponent (left in photos) in a fighting stance (*photo 8-5*).

2. Melvin shifts his weight forward and delivers a Jab at his opponent's head (*photo 8-6*). This forces his opponent to step back out of the way.

3. Before the opponent can step back, "Legs" leaps into the air (*photo 8-7*) and delivers a Reverse Crescent Kick to her head (*photo 8-8*). *Note:* In practice, "Legs" kicks directly over the head of his opponent to avoid making excessive contact and hurting his partner.

8-9

8-10

THOMAS "NICE GUY" OAKES

A newcomer to the East Coast Demo Team, "Nice Guy" is 12 years old and loves to use his hands in fast combinations.

"I've learned one thing since I've gotten into karate and that is it is a lot of hard work and a lot of fun. I especially enjoy the friendship of the team and how everyone works together to help each other out."

Favorite Fight Combinations

Combination One

1. Thomas "Nice Guy" Oakes faces his opponent (left in photos) in a fighting stance (*photo 8-9*).

2. His opponent attempts to punch him in the face. Oakes, seeing the attack, parries it out of the way with the heel of his palm (*photo 8-10*) and quickly delivers a Reverse Punch to his opponent's exposed side (*photo 8-11*).

8-11

8-12

8-13

8-14

Combination Two

1. Oakes faces his opponent (left in photos) in a fighting stance (*photo 8-12*).

2. With his left hand, Oakes grabs his opponent's guard hand (*photo 8-13*) and holds it at opponent's waist level.

3. This creates an opening at opponent's head, which Oakes takes advantage of by throwing a Reverse Punch (*photo 8-14*) for the point.

WILLIE "LITTLE WILLIE" KING

A mighty mite, at age 8, "Little Willie" is a black-belt-level competitor (junior rank). He enjoys mixing gymnastics with his karate techniques.

"To make karate fun, you have to have a good time doing it. That's why I love making up techniques by taking things from my gymnastics and break dancing. I love to watch my opponent's face when I do something he would never expect."

8-15

8-16

8-17

8-18

8-19

8-20

8-21

8-22

Favorite Fight Combinations

Combination One: Cartwheel Kick

1. Willie faces his opponent (left in photos) in a fighting stance (*photo 8-15*).

2. Before his opponent has a chance to "move in on him," as Willie says, Willie places his hands on the floor (*photo 8-16*) and launches himself into a Cartwheel Kick.

3. The first leg, as it comes down from the kick (*photo 8-17*), sets the opponent up by knocking his hands out of the way, so the second kick can come down straight on his head (*photo 8-18*).

Combination Two: Air Walk Kick

1. In a move from break dancing, Willie faces his opponent (left in photos) and faces him in a guard position (*photo 8-19*).

2. Before his opponent can do anything, Willie throws himself to the ground (*photo 8-20*) and launches himself into a handspring or, as break dancers call it, the Air Walk (*photo 8-21*).

3. Willie catches his opponent on the head with his feet on his way down (*photo 8-22*).

MORRIS "BOO" COTTON

At age 12, Morris is a second-degree (junior) black belt and a very accomplished break dancer. Like his teammate "Little Willie," Morris can successfully integrate his break dancing with his karate fighting skills to make a totally unique and personal style of fighting.

"Some people in traditional karate tell me that mixing break dancing with karate is an insult to true karate practice. I don't see it that way. When I fight, I put all I have into it. Break dancing with karate gives me the element of surprise. I'm not out to change karate as a whole; I'm only trying to make a unique personal fighting style. To me, that's what karate is all about."

Favorite Fight Combination

Footwork into Shoulder Roll

1. Morris faces his opponent (right in photos) with a fighting stance (*photo 8-23*).

2. Morris drops to the floor (*photo 8-24*), kicks his opponent's leg out from under him (*photo 8-25*), and turns (*photo 8-26*) to deliver a kick to opponent's head (*photo 8-27*). The moves in photos 26 and 27 are called *footwork* in break dancing.

3. Before his opponent can get up, Morris executes a break-dancing Shoulder Roll (*photos 8-28, 8-29, and 8-30*) to return to a standing position over his opponent (*photo 8-31*). From here, Morris is prepared for the next exchange of techniques.

8-23

8-24

8-25

8-26

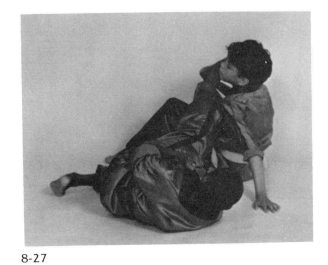

8-27

8-28

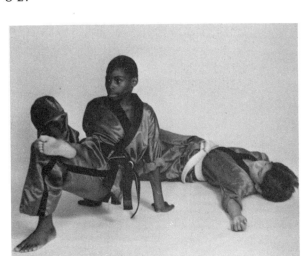

8-29

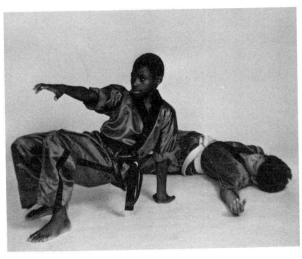

8-30

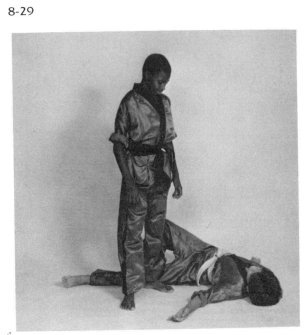

8-31

ABOUT THE AUTHOR

An internationally known writer and authority on the techniques, history, and philosophy of the martial arts, Parulski is the chief instructor at the Yama-Ji School of Traditional Martial Arts in Webster, New York.

A trainer of children and tots (three- to five-year-olds), Parulski holds the following degrees: *yondan* (fourth-degree black belt) in shotokan karate (Japan Karate Association, American Karate Federation); *godan* (fifth-degree black belt) in júdo from the American Society of Classical Judoka; a *yondan* (fourth-degree black belt) in judo from the All-Japan Seibukan Martial Arts and Ways Association; a *menkyo* ("licensed teacher") in aiki-jujutsu (tenshin shin'yo-ryu style) from the Seibukan-kai; a *sandan* (third-degree black belt) in goju-ryu karate (Zen-Nippon Goju-kai and Seibukan-kai); and a white sash in Northern/Southern Shaolin kung-fu and Tai Ch'i Ch'uan.

Parulski is a frequent contributor to *Official Karate Magazine, Inside Karate Magazine, Warriors*, and *Black Belt Magazine*. He is also the author of the following books: *Complete Book of Judo* (Contemporary), *Art of Karate Weapons* (Contemporary), *Secrets of Kung-Fu* (Contemporary), *Taekwon-Do* with Mark McCarthy (Contemporary), *A Path to Oriental Wisdom* (Ohara), *Chinese Therapeutics: Folk Medicine of Kung Fu* (Unique), *Black Belt Judo* (Contemporary), and *The Complete Book of Japanese Swordsmanship* (Paladin Press). Other titles are in preparation.

Currently living in Webster, New York, he directs a martial arts program at St. John Fisher College and is the father of two children, Jackie and Charles. He is the current USA representative for the Dai-Nippon Seibukan Budo/Bugei-kai (All-Japan Seibukan Martial Arts and Ways Association).

ABOUT FRANKIE "DR. SPEED" MITCHELL

Mitchell is the teacher and founder of the East Coast Demo Team, formally known as the Spinning Cobras. A black belt under Aaron Banks (10th dan), Mitchell is a co-founder of the *hatha-goju-ryu* system, a system of karate that combines yoga with classical *Goju-ryu*. He has been featured in *Official Karate Magazine* for his contributions to teaching children.

He currently lives in Syracuse, New York, where he instructs at the Dunbar Center for Children.

ABOUT MAZZOCHETTI KARATE, LTD.

Mazzochetti Karate, Ltd., is one of the most successful schools in the Rochester, New York, area with an enrollment of some 500 students. Debra Mazzochetti, the founder and head teacher of the school, is a *yondan* (fourth-degree black belt) in the isshin-ryu karate system, having initially trained under Joe Jennings and now supervised directly by Master Kichiro Shimabuka (10th dan).

Children appearing in this photo and in the book photos are: FIRST ROW (left to right): David Broddery, Chris Mitchell, and Rob Bodem. SECOND ROW (left to right): Kiarash Foroozesh and Curt Divisser. TOP ROW (left to right): Kids' Instructor Ed Vought, Chief Instructor Debra Mazzochetti, and Maria Mulero.

ABOUT THE EAST COAST DEMO TEAM

The East Coast Demo Team (formally the Spinning Cobras) is a team of highly talented juniors and peewees that compete nationally in fighting (junior/peewee divisions) and kata (traditional and creative).

Enjoying karate for its competitive aspects, the East Coast Demo Team throws everything but the kitchen sink into its performances of karate. Accomplished break dancers, gymnasts, gospel singers, and entertainers, their demonstrations are SRO performances.

They train at the Dunbar Center in Syracuse, New York, under Frankie "Dr. Speed" Mitchell.

Children appearing in this photo and in the book photos are: FIRST ROW (left to right): Dwayne King, Willie King, and Thomas Oakes. MIDDLE ROW (left to right): Sikie Hollimann, Morris Cotton, and Melvin Jamison. TOP ROW: Instructor Frankie Mitchell.

GLOSSARY

Age-uke: Rising Block
Age-zuki: Rising Punch
Choku-zuki: Straight Punch
Chudan: chest area
Chudan Choku-zuki: Mid-Level Straight Punch
Chudan-mae-geri: Mid-Level Front Kick
Chudan soto-uchi: Mid-Level Outside-Inward Block
Dan-zuki: consecutive punching drills
Dojo: karate school
Empi: elbow
Fumikiri: Cutting Kick
Gedan: low-level
Gedan-barai: Low Block
Gi: karate suit
Gyaku-zuki: Reverse Punch
Hachiji-dachi: Open Stance
Haishu: Backhand Strike
Haisoku: instep
Haito: Ridge Hand
Jiyu-kumite: free-fighting (sparring)
Jodan: face area

Jodan Choku-zuki: Face Punch
Jodan Mae-geri: Face-Level Front Kick
Juji-dachi: X Stance
Juji-uke: X Block
Kakato: heel
Kakuto: Bent-Wrist Strike
Karate: way of the empty hand
Kata: formal exercises
Kizumi-zuki: Jab
Kokutsu-dachi: Back Stance
Koshi: ball of the foot
Kumite: sparring
Ma-ai: distance
Mae-geri: Front Kick
Makiwara: striking board
Mawashi-geri: Roundhouse Kick
Migi: right
Musubi-dachi: Informal Stance
Neko-ashi-dachi: Cat Stance
Oi-zuki: Lunging Punch
Sanchin-dachi: Hourglass Stance
Seiken: forefist
Seiken Choku-zuki: Forefist

Straight Punch
Shuto: Knife Hand
Shuto-uchi: Knife-Hand Strike
Sokuto: foot edge
Soto-uke: Outside-Inward Block
Suki: opening (in sparring)
Tameshiwara: board/brick breaking
Tanden: body center (at navel)
Teisho: Palm Heel

Teisho-uchi: Palm-Heel Strike
Teisho-uke: Palm-Heel Block
Tobi-geri: Jumping Kick
Tsuki-waza: punching techniques
Uchi-waza: striking techniques
Ude: forearm
Ushiro-geri: Back Kick
Yoko: side
Yoko-geri: Side Kick
Zen-kutsu-dachi: Front Stance

APPENDIX
KARATE BELT DEGREES

Eighth rank (*hachi-kyu*)—white belt (beginner)

Seventh rank (*shichi-kyu*)—yellow belt (beginner)

Sixth rank (*roku-kyu*)—orange belt (advanced beginner)

Fifth rank (*gokyu*)—green belt, first degree (intermediate)

Fourth rank (*yonkyu*)—green belt, second degree (advanced intermediate)

Third rank (*sankyu*)—brown belt, first degree (beginning advanced)

Second rank (*nikyu*)—brown belt, second degree (intermediate advanced)

First rank (*ikkyu*)—brown belt, first degree (advanced)

DAN (BLACK BELT) LEVELS

Shodan—first degree

Nidan—second degree

Sandan—third degree

Yondan—fourth degree (teacher level)

Godan—fifth degree

Rokudan—sixth degree

Shichidan—seventh degree

Hachidan—eighth degree

Kudan—ninth degree

Judan—tenth degree (master level)

INDEX